Terms and Conditions

LEGAL NOTICE

The Publisher has strived to be as accurate and complete as possible in the creation of this report, notwithstanding the fact that he does not warrant or represent at any time that the contents within are accurate due to the rapidly changing nature of the Internet.

While all attempts have been made to verify information provided in this publication, the Publisher assumes no responsibility for errors, omissions, or contrary interpretation of the subject matter herein. Any perceived slights of specific persons, peoples, or organizations are unintentional.

In practical advice books, like anything else in life, there are no guarantees of income made. Readers are cautioned to reply on their own judgment about their individual circumstances to act accordingly.

This book is not intended for use as a source of legal, business, accounting or financial advice. All readers are advised to seek services of competent professionals in legal, business, accounting and finance fields.

You are encouraged to print this book for easy reading.

Table Of Contents

Foreword

Chapter 1:
Getting Starting In Property Investing

Chapter 2:
Finding Potential Property For Investment

Chapter 3:
Analyzing The Property

Chapter 4:
Buying An Investment Property

Chapter 5:
Overhauling Your Property

Chapter 6:
Strategies In Marketing Your Property

Wrapping Up

Foreword

Property investing is not something to be taken lightly. Careful research and experience should be the important elements exercised in the area of property investing. Get all the info you need here.

Flip'in Cash
Discover the secrets to buy low and sell high in real estate investing

Chapter 1:
Getting Starting In Property Investing

Synopsis

The following are some considerations that should be look into before making the very important decision to be a property investor:

The Basics

Deciding what type of property to invest in makes a lot of difference in how the entire buying exercise plays out. Different types of properties require different types of investing techniques and commitments.

There are also considerations such as property market movements, which will generally affect non landed properties much more than landed ones. This of course not only applies to the sales market but also to the rental markets too.

When considering making purchases, the investor should always try to include a clause in the agreement whereby there are options available and in place to nullify the agreements should the intended property to be purchased is not what it was portrayed to be.

Houses also present a better option for extensions, redesigning and remodeling possibilities and this can add value to the property. With flat, apartment and condo such exercises have limitations and various approvals have to be sought before any work can begin.

Before committing to a purchase the buyer would also need to have a thorough inspection done on the property to ensure its justifying value. Surveying the surrounding area is also something that

should be done as it will defiantly have some bearing on the property value both in the present time and in the future.

Preparing the adequate amount of financing is also something that is important when investing in property. The end result should be favorable to the investor, otherwise the entire exercise would have been wasteful and even worse debt contributing.

Chapter 2:
Finding Potential Property For Investment

Synopsis

There are usually many types of property options available for the discerning investor, and taking the trouble and patience to find such properties will definitely be well worth the effort. It is important however to decide what kinds of real estate investment would most suit the needs and budget of the investor before actually venturing into the actual sourcing for the ideal fit.

Where Is It

There are several popular reasons as to why most investors in the property market make a particular purchase. These may include a purchase for long term rental income, for flip over profits, for long term investment and any other reasons that will contribute to some form of profit for the investor.

Once this has been decided upon then the relevant corresponding properties can be identified and purchased to suit the specific intentions of the investor.

Preparing the finances for such investments, is also something that should be considered extensively as the form of financing used should not eventually cause the investor to be burdened with interest payments that will not make the investment viable after all.

Besides this, having the expert advice of good legal counsel is also a very important service to have. Such counsel, will be able to provide information on the responsibilities of both the owner and the tenant, should the investment be for rental purposes.

Other advice can also be forthcoming through the services of legal counsel, such as the setting up of a company if the investor intends to make more purchases or investments in property.

Another point that most investors find important, is to invest in properties that are within a reasonable distance from the investor. This is to facilitate any transactions or the easy addressing of any problems that may arise after the successful purchase of the property.

Chapter 3:
Analyzing The Property

Synopsis

The process of analyzing the intended returns the property is hoped to gain is done by three very different methods.

They would include the gross yield, the net yield and the actual cash flow yield.

All three methods will effectively show the investor the type of returns that are likely to be enjoyed through the purchase of the intended property.

Therefore before any commitment is made, it would be advantages to conduct any one of these analyzing tactics to ensure a wise investment is done.

Have A Look

Basically the gross yield is where the rental is calculated on a 52 WEEk ratio and then divided by the purchase price. The figure derived from this calculation is the gross yield in percentage.

This is a fairly simple way of making a calculation to deduce if the property will present a viable return.

The net yield however is a little more complicated as it takes into account several different factors before making a suitable calculation on the profits it derives.

Points that are taken into consideration as reflected in the eventual calculations are such as, rates either local or regional whichever one applies, insurance costs, provisions for repairs and maintenance, vacancy periods and other expenses that might be incurred.

Therefore in this scenario the calculations would be based on the weekly rental multiplied by the on year period which is 52 weeks, whereupon the estimated expenses would be deducted from this figure and then the balance would be divided by the cost of the property. The total derived would reflect the percentage of profit yielded.

While the cash flow yield is also just an estimate it portrays a much clearer picture of the true yields when compared to the other two

types. Here the interest rates and other expenses and taxes are also included in the general calculations.

Chapter 4:
Buying An Investment Property

Synopsis

When considering the investment property platform to make money, the individual must be sure that the adequate amounts of funds are available for the purchasing process.

Purchasing

Most investment property forays, involve having to invest and then hold on to the said property for a long term period or when the property value rises to the point where the investor is satisfied with the yield and is ready to sell.

The types of property invested in and the location where the investment is situated all play a pivotal role in ensuring if the investment will eventually yield the desired returns.

Unless the investor has the ready cash it would be rather unwise to invest in this form of property investment as the risks are considerably higher.

If there are inadequate funds then it is very likely that the investor would be saddled with costs instead of profits. Getting expert advice from independent sources that would only have the investor's interest in mind, would help to a certain extent keep looses if any at a minimum.

Because the investment property requires a long term commitment, the investor should be prepared to calculate the cost of ownership.

These may include expenses from owning and managing the property over a long period of time. Some of the expenses would

include property taxes, insurances, utilities, maintenance, vacancies and repairs.

On the plus side there are also tax reliefs and benefits to be enjoyed in this type of investment. At the very least if the property is considered a good buy; the risks the owner is likely to face are comparatively lower than other types of investments with higher risk ratios.

Chapter 5:
Overhauling Your Property

Synopsis

The overhaul exercise need not necessarily be one that incurs high costs and time. With a few adjustments the overhaul experience can be something to be thoroughly enjoyed.

Changing It

The following are some tips to follow in the quest to overhaul the property and yet bust the bank:

- Trying to have some sort of theme in mind, so that there can be some standardized use of material would be very helpful. If the main material is bought in bulk it would be much cheaper and the individual can then apply some level of creatively to each area, to still keep it looking somewhat individualistic in style.

- Conducting a de cluttering exercise maybe all that is needed to create a new look. This style of overhauling will not only be cheaper, but it can also be surprising different, when the eventual look of the room becomes unrecognizable from its original state. Getting rid of everything and then starting out with just the bare necessities from the lot is a good place to start.

- Adding a little color or changing an existing loud color for something more sedate and tranquil will effectively create a new and calmly inviting atmosphere. This is also another cheap way of conducting an overhaul. For those more adventurous a combination of colors can be used. There is even the popular use of motifs to consider when making choices for the overhaul exercise.

- If budget permits, going all out and changing complete sets of furniture should be explored. From bedrooms to kitchens new furniture and fixtures can do wonder toward creating a new look.

- Other larger and more important task that may need serious attention during the overhaul exercise would be the plumbing and wiring of the property. This should be addressed, especially if the property is rather old.

Chapter 6:
Strategies In Marketing Your Property

Synopsis

There are several ways to create interest in the property on the market to ensure enough visibility to lock in a sale. The more interest the property attracts, the better the chances of it being sold or rented in a short span of time.

Great Info

The following are some strategies that can be employed in order to create this visibility and attraction:

- Making a list of all the special feature that make the property stand out or be different from others around, should be done. Included in this list should be elements that would be an attractive selling point and also hard to resists. Highlighting negative elements that definitely don't exist in this property will also portray to the prospective client, what they can avoid and thus benefit by committing to a deal on the property.

- Once the list is drawn up, then the target audience attention should be actively sought and the points should be extensively advertised to ensure the desired impact of curiosity and interests are firmly established. Using captions that would personally impact and play on the prospective client's perceptions and ideals would be beneficial.

- Talking to anybody and everybody would also help to create the free publicity for the marketing of the said property. This has been known to be an effective way of getting the required attention that eventually brings forth a successful sale.

- If time and energy permits, having an open house or garage sale will also be another effective way to get the attention of interested parties. This is an ideal way of informing everyone in the area about the property being available for sale or rent depending on the owner's requirements. People attending the garage sale can also act as advertising instruments to spread the word about the availability of the property.

Wrapping Up

If the investor is looking for a good source of passive income, then this sort of investment would be ideal both in the present and for future income in the retirement phase.

www.ingramcontent.com/pod-product-compliance
Lightning Source LLC
Chambersburg PA
CBHW030603220526
45463CB00007B/3154